"SMALL BUSINESS"

YOU DON'T NEED *CAPITAL* TO GET STARTED!

Grace Faiz Evans

"Small Business"

You Don't Need Capital To Get Started!

ISBN: 978-0-9872592-4-0

All scriptures herein are taken from the NIV Zondervan Publishing House 1973-1984 Edition

For more information or to order additional copies contact:

Grace Evans
www.youdontneedcapital.com

Table of Contents

FORWARD

I have known Grace for 20 years, and since day one, she has amazed and impressed me beyond any person that I've ever known.

When you talk with Grace, you know instantly that she is literally 'one in a million'. The more you listen to her, the more you want to know her.

I have learned that if Grace says something can be done, then it is a project to run with. She puts effort, investigation and effervescence into every project which she is involved in.

Grace exudes the confidence of one who knows exactly who she is, what you and she are capable of, and where you are both headed.

'Passionate' is a word which under-values the power of Grace. Once you've met her, you'll never forget her, and you'll always trust her.

This book is so well designed that anyone will be able to start a business by simply following the steps which Grace has set out. We all have good ideas, and this book will inspire you to put them into practice so that you can, and will, run your own business.

I thank God for Grace.

Sharon Millward, Author (2011)

ACKNOWLEDGEMENT

This book is an acknowledgment and gratitude to God. The one who created each one of us uniquely and individually by ***Design*** and not ***Default*** in His image, purpose filled, to fulfill our predetermined **DESTINY** and leave behind a profound **LEGACY!**

“SMALL BUSINESS”

YOU DON’T NEED *CAPITAL* TO GET STARTED!

Grace Faiz Evans

CHAPTER 1

Your Business Niche

"Good business leaders create a vision,
articulate the vision,
passionately own the vision,
and relentlessly drive it to completion"

-Jack Welch-

Specialize in a niche market and you will grow your enterprise exponentially!

What is this book about? It is about enterprise directed to change your business prospects. It is about a U-turn in your thinking, directed to the betterment of your life and those you interact with. It is an invitation for you to delve into the art of the possible because you are reality, and a possibility come true. You are reality because fundamentally there was a creator with a vision, a dream-seed to create you in His image and endow you with His creative genes to fulfill the same purpose of being creative. Your purpose is to defy the mundane in order to produce a new vision or dream-seed, which will transform your business world and those who interact with it.

This knock on your door is to awaken you, and make you aware of the potential within you to create a new environment by developing a vision, a dream-seed, and to teach you how to grow this dream-seed, by taking control of your circumstances, promoting your self-development to advance your self-discovery.

The aim is to encourage you to dig out the vision from within yourself and find your intrinsic value, because in you lays great potential to make a difference in your life and those around you. This book is stating the art of the possible because others have done it. Why not you? You could be one of those history makers like Moses, Joshua, Martin Luther King Jr., Mother Teresa, Einstein, and Gandhi. People created in the image of God who used God's creative potential in them, formed a vision for their lives and got off their backside to activate their dream-seed, planned and worked at it and made a difference in the world. The greatest book ever written, the Bible, specifically states that without a vision the people perish.

Activate your desire to seek out and find your dream-seed, a vision in your business life. Once you find your dream-seed, then it becomes your responsibility to ignite this dream, put a work-plan to it, follow that plan regardless of how many times you fall, knowing that at the end of the day you will achieve your goal.

The information provided in this book will not be leaving you with words of encouragement only, but also providing you with a course of action and knowledge of how to navigate through the unknown. It is providing you with leads, a light to direct your steps into unknown territory where only some have gone before. Technical leads that will assist you to emerge on the other side realising your dream-seed and transforming your personal life and those dependent on you and around you.

Finally, this book is telling you ***have a vision, have a dream-seed, give it a go while you can, and the sky will be the limit.*** Promote your circumstances by grasping the fundamental that even with no money to begin a business, it is possible to generate wealth if you have a vision, a dream, an idea. People will always follow those with a vision, a dream-seed, and men and women with a vision. A dream-seed will always be a history-maker.

Guidance is provided in this book, for you, to realize the potential within you to transform yourself and influence your environment by stepping out and rising above the noise, allowing your imagination to see and taste success!

Now, you have the opportunity to become a history-maker.

> ***"Good business leaders***
> ***create a vision,***
> ***articulate the vision,***
> ***passionately own the vision,***
> ***and relentlessly drive it to***
> ***completion"***
>
> ***Jack Welch***

CHAPTER 2

Who We Are
and our purpose in life

"The basic rule of free enterprise: you must give, in order to get"

-Scott Alexander-

Small business enterprise is becoming one of the largest growing communities worldwide as more and more people look for ways to better themselves, their circumstances, their lifestyle, retire early and generally get out of the nine to five grind. People have become dissatisfied with earning an income through their job and are looking for ways to earn the mighty dollar through other avenues which better suit their individuality and purpose, such as investments or business entrepreneurship.

By embracing this growing frustration of trying to achieve or find one's business purpose or calling in life, it is noted that those who pursue it actually begin moving towards their called destiny. This leads them to their ultimate destination and that is true life fulfillment!

To be satisfied or fulfilled in life, we as humans do one thing in common and that is ***"search"***. We search, we hunt down what we desire, or are determined to get, or achieve. It is known that we are hunters and gatherers, so we use our God given natural skills to do just that. We gather friendships, acquire information, create comfort in our lives, provide for our children, and have the best of what our money can buy, always striving to achieve the calling for a long and supposedly satisfying life.

Our calling is simply knowing who we are, understanding our makeup, and most importantly knowing our dreams and desires that are bubbling away inside of us. We have a common thread with one and all, and that is fear. Fear of the unknown, fear of knowing that we can fail and are no different to those who have tried and failed. But we never seem to take into account the ones that made it to the top through sheer determination, commitment and focus. I ask the question, why not take the risk of rising above, and if you fall, rise again until you see your vision transform into a reality?

I am sure at some stage of our walk in life we have all tried to succeed, determined to rise above, and have fallen gracefully or even ungracefully. However, to succeed requires ***achievement of something desired, planned, or attempted***. I encourage you to let those words sink in. The achievement of something ***desired***, ***planned*** or ***attempted***. That's why we must rise again and again until we fulfill our desires.

> *"Know where to find the information and how to use it. That 's the secret of success"*
>
> **Albert Einstein**

Chance -vs- Design

We all know that it's not by chance that we exist. We are created by God, a mastermind artistic entrepreneur, who called this world into existence and moulded us from the dust of the earth. A potter, who mixed the clay by using the exact measurements with much needed water to smooth the imperfections, God kneaded the product until the right consistency not just looked good, but felt good, having strength and revealing character, ready to be moulded and worked into a perfected piece of art for display, to be admired.

We are the product of the process of creation, which is very well thought through. It is planned for an end result, with a vision in mind. It would only be a matter of time before the potter would sit back and admire the work of his hands and enjoy the fruit of his labour. It is perfect! The end result is achieved. The product sells!

We also have a process that is inbred into our DNA which we can develop into a product. This is because the same composition which was used to make us also dwells within us. We have the responsibility of extracting the result/s (product) from within, and have it work in synergy with other results (products), so the world goes around and around, leaving a legacy, a blueprint for the next generation. This then becomes our personal responsibility to share, equip and train our successors in the present and next generations.

As a child, my father used to travel overseas at least once a year. Working closely with government departments, he was assigned the job of training other nations on how to control certain weeds that either took over farming lands or in some cases acted as a parasite in forests and eradicated good trees which nature needed. Before his travels we would all prepare a shopping list for Dad so he would return with goodies for us. At the time, the country we resided in did not have much food let alone treats such as sweets and chocolates. To buy treats you had to go to the black market and pay foreign currency which was just out of the question, as all the money spent aided the military for the ongoing civil war.

So, we all made the most of it. My list always contained consumables such as chocolates, sweets, crisps and practicals such as toothpaste. I never had toys on my list. On this one particular list, my brother had a snooker cue amongst other things and I remember thinking that there was no way Dad would spend that kind of money on my brother and besides, it's too long to fit in a suitcase. Well, I was wrong! He got his snooker cue and all the other goodies as well.

A month after Dads return all the great tasting treats that were brought back from overseas for my siblings were devoured and not even the smell was left. I on the other hand had carefully wrapped up all my goodies and stashed them in the back of my cupboard, waiting for the opportune time to open my 'shop' on my bed, having pillows as my fortress so my brother could not pinch anything without me knowing. My 'shop' would open when my uncle was around as my brother would spend all his saved up pocket money on my 'shop' and sweet talk my uncle and mother into giving him more money to buy from my desirable selection.

My goodies would be sold sometimes three months after Dad's return and up to six months. The older the product the more expensive it became. Not because it had passed its due date, but because there was now less product available and therefore it became a wanted commodity.

Let's just say in a nutshell, my savings account was very healthy. Yes I desired to eat those things as well, but my greater passion was to save and buy myself a gold ring. My reward was far too valuable to be tempted by temporary highs, so focus became my goal.

When you have sight, you have power. A vision of where you are heading and what you want to accomplish is the most powerful free gift we all possess. It's just a matter of activating it. Life has a way of deactivating our visions and unfortunately side-tracking us with distractions. Stay focused!

> ***"Patience, articulation, planning, assessment, structure, time-lines, strategic actions, leads to the pathway of a successful business venture, be it a service or product"***
>
> **Grace Faiz Evans**

To create an enterprise we must first find the seed, our purpose..........

I call this a dream-seed, which is deposited in one's heart and develops as one takes time to ponder on it and search it out.

The key for any enterprise is to create a pathway to allow the dream-seed to materialize by utilizing the skills one already has. These skills are called tools or implements that will promote your dream-seed. This dream-seed is planted in your heart. Note, I said *heart* and not *mind*! We all know that out of the heart come the issues of life. It is with our mind that we make the decision, but it is with our heart that we choose our course. It is through the furnace of adversities of which our heart ponders on, that solutions are created.

My husband decided after 5 years of marriage to uproot and move from the City to a Country Town where the population was under ten thousand people. At first I thought it was the craziest, illogical, insensitive idea my husband came up with as we had mortgages, and secure jobs to fund those mortgages. I nicely explained to my loving husband that a small country town would not provide good paying jobs and, besides, the locals of any town become the priority for positions before new settlers.

My husband did not know how it was to happen but he was adamant and felt a peace about the move as he thought it would better us and give us a lifestyle to enjoy each other's company, rather than the rushed life we had been living. As crazy as I thought he was for considering such a *thought*, it provided me with a challenge to attempt and resolve, and to explore the unknown risks and opportunities which may eventuate from such a decision.

An approach had to be considered - housing, regular income, tenants in our vacated home, temporary residence for us to reside until we understood how the town worked before we invested in our new home, types of industries and availability of work etc. This was a mammoth job, but my husband knew that if I put my mind to anything I would find a way to make things happen if all the figures stacked up.

I will write a whole book on this story one day to show what goal setting and planning can do, but to give a brief, we relocated within one month of the decision being made, secured work, and started our first business within three weeks of our arrival. Our second business took off after six months and we continued to grow in stature, finances and favour within the small community. We no longer were trading time for money but time for value. I learnt another valuable lesson from this decision that someone other than me made. Trust those that come to you with a vision or an idea. Explore it, do your due diligence, your feasibility, and determine if stepping out in faith will give you a return and a tangible reward. Then go for it!

Our mind tends to be the battleground of self-doubt, confusion, worry, rejection, distraction, depression and anger. If we only used our mind, we would doubt and procrastinate, until we miss the opportunity of discovering our purpose (dream-seed) in life.

It is only when you find your purpose (dream-seed) that you will find your power..........

When you withstand the challenges and adversities in life, sometimes you will find the instrument which will promote you to your fullest capacity. You can *sometimes* determine what is going *to* happen to you, however, you can *always* determine what is going to happen *in* you, and the result of your actions will speak louder than words.

The second year into our marriage I approached my husband and told him that I thought it was time to expand our property portfolio as I had just received a small pay rise. So after a few discussions of sorting out our fears and the 'what ifs' I researched the market nationally and studied demographics, council approved development plans etc. We also tossed around the idea of another stream of income to supplement should one of us becomes incapable of bringing in an income.

I knew deep down inside that expanding our self like a rubber band might either snap us or stay stretched, in which case we can try stretching it further in the future, but for now I needed to ensure that all our ducks were in a row. We explored monetizing a hobby that my husband had for ourselves to provide extra cash, and I looked at a positively geared property knowing that the hobby could turn into a profitable business down the track and we could offset the extra income to interest expenses to reduce our income tax at the same time pay off the principle in the property.

So, the challenge was now complete and it was a done deal! We monetized my husband's hobby, which was making custom fishing lures targeting specific species of fish, and I found a positively geared property securing a two year rental lease, and so our journey began in the world of property investments.

When we use our heart, we begin to exercise our vision and passion which provides purpose and comfort when facing life's adversities. We begin to dream and visualise a solution for our problem, which in turn delivers reassurance and comfort.

Desire and passion reveal a person's character and promotes their circumstances. It is not possible to reveal the true attitude of a person or show their character until adversity strikes. The circumstances of life can bury us, but a positive attitude can use the circumstances for success.

What you think, determines the course of your life..........

You are the one with the free will. You are the one who shapes your future. You are the one with the ultimate decision making authority. The choice is yours, even if it is not natural to you, you still choose! "Free will" can either promote you or condemn you. There is a plan and purpose for your life and it is your responsibility to find out who you are. Find your value and you will find your predetermined destiny. I challenge you today to protect the most treasured organ in your human temple, which is your heart.

Without it you will not be able to control your attitude or course in life. It is your rudder because it is built and installed to steer your ship.

A wise saying by King Solomon that I find true to any business venture I commit myself to, and allows me to focus on the goal and eliminate distractions, is a proverb that says:

***"Above all else,
guard your heart
for it is the well spring
of life"***

**Proverbs 4:23
King Solomon**

How true! Your heart is known as being the well spring of life. Out of the heart flows purpose, compassion, attitude, character, and desire to stand firm. Your desire is your treasure that is locked up in the depth of your being. Once activated, you will stand firm and walk upright, focused with determination and commitment to reach your goal. It is well known that pursuit is the proof of your desire. Determine and possess what you are willing to pursue!

I would like to take a few moments to elaborate on a dream-seed. A dream is having visions pass through your mind. ***"Dreams can often make a creative thought occur to the person or give a sense of inspiration".***

A dream is like a seed that is deposited in us. The seed multiplies over time and is sitting in a basket in the back of your mind. Every now and then your mind activates this seed. You chew on the thought for a few hours, maybe a day or two and then return it to its rightful place, the basket! The thoughts continue to remain dormant until you decide to take authority over them.

Back in the days when I was working for an employer, I remember being very discontented with my employer, not with the work as I loved the work, but with my employer who seemed to take advantage of my hard working ethics and take the work off the others in my team who struggled to get through their quota and have me do their work so that we all supposedly received a bonus at the end of the month for achieving the forecasted budget. May I add that no bonus was ever received as the budget kept growing through the month as I neared the finish line!

I knew that if I allowed my attitude to sour then I would be of no benefit to the employer or myself. So, I decided to find a way out of this situation because the same treatment I have received from the current employer was the same treatment I received from other employers after only being employed for less than six months.

Deep soul searching began and problem solving is one of my greatest assets. I began an unusual journey which to this day is serving me well.

I selectively chose employers whom I thought were small enough to allow me to make an impact to their bottom line through my creativity and hard work. I drafted a letter, attached my Resume' and faxed it through. I must admit I had some doubt deep down inside, but I kept reassuring myself that if it is not meant to be then no harm is done, I will however try and try and try till I find an open door.

My phone rang hot for a week, with requests of appointments. As you can imagine I was so elated and needed time to calm down before I could make a strategic plan of why I had accepted an interview with them. I spent two solid days interviewing employers. Note, I was interviewing them not the other way around. I had control of the situation because my skills were in demand so I leveraged the opportunity and provided information about myself, qualifications and experience.

The end result was instead of me choosing ***one*** employer out of all who wanted me, I concluded that contracting my services was going to allow me to capitalize and grow in experience rapidly because I knew that my work ethics promoted value everywhere I went. Out of adversity a solution was birthed, and freedom of releasing me as a captive from an employer, who took advantage of my hard working ethics, was a battleground won!

The dream-seed needs to be activated and used with purpose, for an expected return..........

How you may ask? We read about the potter who invested his time in developing his passion, his deposited seed, and his dream. It was his talent and passion to be creative, artistic and bring to reality a vision of what could be done with a clay pot, and what it could look like. He also envisioned the pot being one of the best masterpieces he ever created. Each pot he made was made with love, diligence, excellence and perfection. The time invested was his free capital which returned praise in the form of trade.

The potter strategically designed this one pot to perform many aspects of service for those that viewed its splendour with admiration. The technical, calculated and measured pot was going to be of service for water being stored and kept cool, or as a centrepiece vase displaying itself with an added touch of flowers, or as a carrier of life drawing water from a well. This product was to be multi-purposed and like no other. Its beauty would glisten and resonate in the eye of the beholder.

Everything that rises from within us rises from a bountiful spring of love and service to others, birthing a solution and becoming an answer to many.......

This potter created value out of clay. His hands worked a solution to meet many needs. His dream of being of great service to his community and benefit to others was fulfilled, and transformed ***his*** vision into a reality.

This book will teach you the principles of starting an enterprise with NO Capital. However, it is specifically designed for those who are givers, in particular those who have a heart for service, those who live for bettering others and being a blessing by promoting excellence to fellow humans. It is about understanding and experiencing one's well spring of life which emanates from one's innermost being and cries out louder than one's decisions. It is called a conscience, which is the soul of mankind. The well-spring of life speaks of knowledge, skill and ability and through the attributes of perception and attitude, you will be able to create wealth.

We are called to be of service to others. If you are reading this book and thinking that you want to make a wad of money anyway possible, through small business, starting with NO capital, then I am sorry to burst your bubble, but this is probably not the right book for you!

Service to others is the primary seed everyone should possess……

It is not something that can be bought, but an action taken by an individual who is summoned to be a solution to the world. It must be activated from within so it can manifest in reality.

To be successful you need to provide what others want, something that would be of benefit to others……

For example, if you have an apple seed, you will notice that the seed is dry and DEAD. The seed is dormant and it is only ONE seed. This seed, in order for it to produce fruit, must germinate by being placed in soil that is conducive to a favourable environment to allow it to grow and develop to maturity, to bear fruit and fulfill its destiny.

Effort is now required to water the seed, nourish it and develop it until you start to see fruit. The fruit then produces multiple seeds, called compound interest, which allows you to plant an orchard resulting in abundant fruit, called the harvest, which can then be sold for a profit. It takes effort and time to bring your dream-seed to reality or maturity.

Now that we understand the process of planting and harvesting a seed, let us look at this from a business perspective. The seed is your vision, your creative dream, your aspiration, your desire and your passion. At some stage in life the issues of life, including distractions, stagnates and stunts our desires.

Consequently, the dream-seed becomes dormant but keeps crying out *Activate me! Activate me!* Basically, it cries out louder when adversity strikes. But, we are well conditioned to suppress those feelings and those desires because they are wasteful energy and we cannot possibly see how we can channel those desires into something productive or fruitful.

To extract the seed or dream from within you, you must have the right partnerships, the right support, the right coach, the right mentor and of course the right fertile environment……

First, you need to identify the source of your dream. We all know how to distinguish between good and bad dreams. Not all dreams are good and it is your responsibility to rule out the dreams that are born out of brokenness, and dreams that are born out of bad beginnings. *These dreams are trying to prove something to people around you. These are not good dreams.* They are nightmares! They end in agony and despair because they were not born correctly. These dreams are born out of fleshly issues and problems that take hold of your life. They are born out of strife, to prove something to somebody who might not ever change their mind and opinion of you in the first place! You cannot allow somebody's opinion of you to become your motivation. You have got to rule out dreams of being seen, being heard, being recognised, being different and being impressive just to be accepted.

A good dream is one that knows its environment. Knows to find the right soil to allow it to grow, feed and be directed with positive counsel and a forward approach. It's all around us, we just need to look for it.

To move into your dream purpose, you need to do the most important thing, of allowing yourself to dream the right dream………

Don't kill your dreams because you have grown deaf to your inner voice and blind to your opportunities. To find the right dream-seed, you need to embrace the fact that you are a dreamer and it is okay to be pregnant with ideas and on a mission to deliver. Dreams are ideas of the subconscious and can often make a creative thought or be a sense of inspiration.

So embrace something ***New*** today, something ***Fresh*** and something ***Significant*** and allow it to take shape in your life! Untangle yourself so you can live out your purpose and live out that dream with a sense of fulfillment. Liberate yourself and feel those chains of bondage fall off. Feel free to express yourself, free to discover yourself, free to move into avenues that are controversial. Find the seed within you that you need to sow today to reap the harvest tomorrow. It's never too late, you can start now!

Do you know what your dream-seed is?

If you do, take a moment to write it down.

CHAPTER 3

Wealth Creation

"All riches have their origin in mind.
Wealth is in ideas not money"

-Robert Collier-

There is a parable of a sower in the greatest book ever written, the Bible. The parable says that *"a farmer went out to sow his seed. As he was scattering the seed, some fell along the path and the birds came and ate it up. Some fell on rocky places, where it did not have much soil; it sprang up quickly because the soil was shallow. But when the sun came up, the plants where scorched and they withered because they had no root. Other seed fell on good soil, it came up, grew and produced a crop, multiplying thirty, sixty or even a hundred times"* (Mark 4:3-8).

We learn from this parable that if your soil (your environment) is not prepared and does not have boundaries then your dream-seed will fall on deaf ears and be crushed by those you call 'close alliances', or it will fall on rocky places where it will take shallow root and not go far. You will have the encouragement you need to get started but it will not continue when fruit is not evident in the short-term.

You see, the farmer had some seed fall on good soil. The seed produced a good crop which was bountiful. All of us are susceptible to acceptance of negativity and positivity and we must exercise the authority we have to protect our dream-seed, then focus and create a pathway through the adversities we are challenged with, so a solution is birthed. The solution will bring an abundance that we can sustain, and thereby develop our God given ability.

To succeed in life we must seek direction, prepare ourselves, work hard and invest in the right things..........

Material success is only part of the story and not really of great importance. The real objective is to become a channel through which you can bless others with your service or product and become fulfilled in what you do. Wealth will follow close behind. Notice the sequence in the story of the farmer. He had a strategy. He knew that God did not create anything without seed inside itself.

The seed determines the end from the beginning. There is something inside all of us that is able to pollinate and cross-pollinate. It is self-producing and self-perpetuating. If you discover what is in you then everything around you will begin to change through the power of self-discovery. The hidden treasure is locked up inside you. You and I will never be able to dictate our circumstances unless we take inventory of what is hidden inside of us.

Visualize yourself as one who is so needed, that the whole creation is waiting for you to ***discover*** your responsibility. Challenge yourself to develop a solution for them!

The farmer who was self-employed knew that consistent sowing guaranteed consistent reaping. Each seed planted scheduled a harvest. The farmer is providing a solution to his communities needs. He is also providing an income for his family, which in turn would give him skills to train his family in, as well as giving a future for his children and an inheritance.

We are responsible for making the right decisions today to influence our future tomorrow……….

Do you want to make a difference in your life and the lives of others?

Effort is required to bring your dream to reality.........

It takes effort to get to where you want to go. Dare to dream beyond your dreams!

Once you catch the vision, (the dream-seed) you will then be commissioned to decide what your assignment will be, what goals and plans need to be put in place to achieve your purpose and your calling, to be the light and salt to your environment, your industry, your place of employment, your community and the world.

Before you have provision, you first and foremost must have VISION!.........

"Where there is no vision the people perish"

Proverbs 29:18
King Solomon

What I find interesting with King Solomon's wisdom is that he realizes, without PEOPLE there is no vision. The key is to have willing people. People who have hope and faith in seeing their dreams come true. However, this is not for the faint-hearted. This requires commitment, determination, and a resilient spirit to stand strong and move forward birthing ones dream to make it a reality!

CHAPTER 4

Wealth Creation Formula

"Wealth is the product of a man's capacity to think."

-Ayn Rand-

Now, I am sure I have your attention with such a title! Wealth creation is a simple formula.

The greatest secret to wealth creation is discipline, focus and determination, which produces success..........

Recently, I heard of a great speaker who came a long way from Canada to visit a local country town in North Queensland, Australia. The country town is literally a dot on a map in a remote area. To visit this farming town, one must fly in and then drive three hours north from the nearest airport through a steep range. I personally found this incomprehensible that such a profound speaker was secured to bring outstanding teachings and business entrepreneurship skills to such a remote area. It baffled my thoughts. At first I did not think this was true until I telephoned the organisers and my doubts were laid to rest that this was a reality and the speaker had already arrived that day.

Because I had followed some of the principles of this speaker, I wanted more than anything to meet this great person of power. More importantly, to spend 15 minutes with this honourable person who made inroads and an impact on people's lives, nationally and internationally. I thought it would be a great privilege to be able to glean from this person's experience. You see, I had cultivated my soil and was prepared to take any measures to associate with the right people and network with the right communities even if it meant travelling extensive distances. This was a splendid opportunity at my door step, and I was going to chase my destiny and those that influence my rightful business decisions. Needless to say, it was an awe inspiring time and what I learnt is already producing harvest!

I encourage you to create your world, create your surroundings, and make sure your environment is conducive to your sustained growth.

The right environment for your dream is to spend time with other dreamers who have vision.........

You ask why? When you hang around other dreamers, they are highly likely to produce the environment necessary for your dream-seed to grow and multiply.

Imagination is a powerful gift and, without imagination we would not develop new products.........

The world has so much creative power which has come through people who have activated the creative gift, imagination. Dr. Martin Luther King envisioned a world where people of all races would one day be united and not judged by the ***"colour of their skin but by the content of their character"***. Adolf Hitler also had a vision. He envisioned a nation of pure Aryan race, and eventually a world of pure line Germanic decent. Both men had vision and both pursued their vision. They impacted society, but only one of those visions obviously benefited the entire world.

Both began with an IDEA, a thought and imagination..........

It's simple, *if you don't think anything you don't get anything!* Your desires and passions create your visions. The vision of your idea is ***transformational*** and the truth is ***transactional*** when you step out in faith and make it happen. You have to have the faith to activate something that has not even happened yet!

> *"Now faith is the substance of things hoped for, the evidence of things not seen"*
>
> **Hebrews 11:1**

When you see the invisible you can do the impossible..........

Faith is the transport. It is the instrument to obtaining your wildest dreams. Your dream-seed is in a state where it has untapped potential. The right environment allows it to grow and mature to what it needs to produce. Have the faith to tap into your potential and explore your hidden treasures.

Key Principles to Establish Your Wealth Creation (Dream-Seed):

- ***POWER - Choose Your Environment:***
  Introduce the dream-seed to the right environment and it will naturally bring *increase!*

- ***PROCESS - Personal-Development:***
  Water the seed, fertilise it with good nutrients, nourish your established roots and allow the right people to speak into your life while you are still establishing your goals and plans. Use coaches, mentors, many advisors who have walked the walk before you, glean from their experiences and expand your sphere of knowledge.

- ***PRESERVATION - Ground Your Roots:***

> Your tree can only produce fruit when you plant yourself by streams of living water. That simply means to have the right input flowing into your life daily. Associate with the right people, read the right books, develop your intellect and advance your passion in the area your vision is leading you to ***daily!***

This simple process allows you to receive a transfer of intellectual wealth from those you choose to surround yourself with. It will create a new season for you and allow you to operate in the zone.

Once you are in the zone you will naturally innovate. Innovation is the key to wealth creation ....

Being in the zone is having total focus on what we can create so as to provide a solution to our environment. We generally find that deep soul searching often provides us with many clues and lots of ideas. Hobbies, talents, passions, and desires, all derive from within our soul. We are uniquely and wonderfully made and every part of us resonates with wanting to excel and achieve all that life has in store for us by creating our world. This I call well springs of life, that rise from within.

These well springs bubble over with innovation and creativity delivering a revelation to you of how to create a product, process or provide a service that will be of great worth, and produce added value both financially and emotionally.

So activate your dream-seed today……

Allow it to give you a revelation of information and then strategize that innovative information. Write it down as goals and start working on it every day. Challenge yourself to create a solution and implement it. Introduce it into the marketplace so you may enjoy the fruits of your labour.

CHAPTER 5

The Season

"To everything there is a season, and a time
to every purpose under the heaven"

-Ecclesiastes 3:1 - King Solomon-

Seasons are equally as important as your dream-seed..........

You cannot be a farmer and just decide to plant a crop whenever you like. A farmer takes into account the seasons and when he can plant and when he can harvest. Our seasons are dictated by the sun, moon and stars.

Strategically plant your dream-seed in the right season and begin to develop it.........

For example, if you owned a sugar cane farm you would know that you need to prepare your land and sow your crop in Winter and Autumn in anticipation of the Summer rains. When summer arrives, the crop will grow, and be strong enough not to be damaged by the heavy rain but instead benefit from it. The heavy rains will water and grow the plant without much expense to the farmer.

It is also common knowledge that rain carries more nutrients than deep spring water. Therefore, the farmer can be assured of good sugar content in his crop before harvest time. Similarly, if you had a paper recycling business, you would start the business either at the beginning of an accounting fiscal year or after the first quarter of any new year.

Firstly, if you start it in the new fiscal year you will be assured of more comprehensive financial reporting figures and it is also the beginning of new budgets handed down and being released.

Secondly, if you start after the first quarter of a fiscal year, you are also assured that a clear direction and financial plan has grounded itself in any business structure and decisions can be made on the spot. For example, budgets are allocated to certain departments and plans are put in place for large and small business structures for strategic growth. Therefore business spending is invested in training, paper recycling or so many dollars are set aside for donations or fund raisers etc.

Every country has different business rules. However, the basics of starting a business foundation correctly are universal and therefore your strategies should include;

Five (5) Strategic Points in Establishing a New Enterprise:

1. **Goals**

   Goals are dreams with a deadline. Set down goals you must achieve each day to reach your destination. This is heavy lifting and only your passion will keep you moving towards this deadline.

2. **Planning**

   Write your vision, your dream-seed down so you can read it every day and speak it into being. What you say you will see, it's the Law of Attraction. You must have the faith that you have given birth to an idea. Write it down! This is called a Business Plan.

3. **Objectives**

   Write your business objectives, which are the practical steps needed to help you achieve your short, intermediate, and long-term goals.

4. **Activities**

   Are you doing all you could be, not just passing time but spending time meaningfully and promoting your personal development by enhancing your understanding? You must apply yourself and do your due diligence.

5. Tasks

Create a to-do list and 'project manage' your performance.

To be able to achieve the strategic points noted in 'Establishing a New Enterprise' you must have a deep conviction of your vision, and a driving passion with a **"*go-getter*"** mentality and a **"*can-do*"** attitude. These are the two key ingredients to a successful business. Without them it will simply be a recipe for failure.

CHAPTER 6

Strategic Point No. 1

Goals

"Without goals and plans to reach them, you are like a ship that has set sail with no destination."

-Fitzhugh Dodson-

A business can be registered and started anytime during a fiscal year..........

However, if you have attended to the pointers in the previous chapter of, goal-setting, planning, objectives, activities and tasks, then *goal-setting* will be the first point to be addressed.

Start your goal setting by contacting one of the governing bodies available on the following page, depending on your country of origin. This can be found on www.worldwide-tax.com. The government bodies will give you an outline of what requirements are needed to start a sole trading, family partnership, discretionary trust or limited liability company. Depending on your plans *it would be best to start small as a sole trader and revise the setup after three quarters of the fiscal year.* If you can see that you are just breaking ground then stick to your current tax registration.

However, if you feel your turnover will attract over fifteen percent tax, then I would suggest speaking with an Accountant and they can revise your set-up and advise you on your growing needs. If you are not happy with the info they provide, then acquire the information and go back to the Tax Authority and change or re-register yourself.

This process is crucial, so ask as many questions as possible and cover your bases before choosing a registration.

"Without goals and plans to reach them,
you are like a
ship that has set sail
with no destination"

Fitzhugh Dodson-

World Tax Revenue Administrations

Albania Taxation Department	www.tatime.gov.al
Argentina Ministry of Finance	www.mecon.gov.ar
Armenia Tax Service	www.taxservice.am
Austria Ministry of Finance	www.bmf.gv.at
Australian Taxation Office	www.ato.gov.au
Bangladesh Board of Revenue	www.nbr-bd.org
Barbados Inland Revenue	www.barbados.gov.bb
Belgium Fiscal Administration	www.fiscus.fgov.be
Brazil Ministry of Finance	www.receita.fazenda.gov.br
Bulgaria Tax Administration	www.taxadmin.minfin.bg
Canada Revenue Agency	www.cra-arc.gc.ca
China	www.satc.gov.cn
Croatia Tax Administration	www.porezna-uprava.hr
Cyprus	www.mof.gov.cy
Czech Ministry of Finance	www.mfcr.cz
US Internal Revenue Service	www.irs.gov

These worldwide tax offices may have different titles such as Tax Administration, Tax Office, Tax Service, Tax Authority, Tax Board etc. Often Tax Administrations have a different title, for example, Inland Revenue, Revenue Service or Revenue Authority. In some countries the Tax Administration web site is a part of the Ministry of Finance.

These websites will give you the option of registering your business details and obtaining a business number so you can start trading.

It is also advisable to contact the relevant directory and ask these questions……

- Q **Can I register on line or do I need to attend a branch?**
- Q **Will this Business Registration Number be sufficient for me to trade or do I need to register with another governing body to obtain a Legal Business Name as well?**
- Q **What other information do I need to prepare for registration?**
- Q **What are my responsibilities and obligations?**
- Q **When can I start trading? Can it be immediate or will I have to wait for official notification from the Tax Office?**

Generally you will find the Tax Office to be very helpful. They will provide you with brochures, flyers and inundate you with emails. Why? *Because you have now registered to becoming a tax collector for the tax office!* We all need to pay taxes and the way the system is set up, shows that, it does not matter who you are, you will still have to declare your income and expenses and lodge activity statements. It's a self-audit system and they are willing to trust you with such details because you have legally approached them and provided your personal details to start trading.

Bear in mind that it is good to plan and know when the Fiscal Year begins, for accounting purposes..........

If you start right, you end well. Always plan and prepare, knowing that if you have well maintained organized bookwork, *accountants will love you and you will love yourself!*

Record-keeping provides accurate financial reporting and also assists futuristically if you present a business plan to the bank or a prospective partnership showing continual growth in your financial quarters and annually. It is imperative to start the race right at the appointed time and establish your eminence, your good relationships, with all governing bodies and the marketplace.

On the following page you will find a chart showing the beginning and the end of a Financial Year in different countries. Depending on where you are going to establish your enterprise, plan your timing to enter the market right.

I encourage you to study the Tax Office website of choice. It is not a daunting process, quite the opposite. It is quite liberating as it enlightens you with what you can and can't do.

I believe understanding these sites is the key element of why the rich get richer and the poor get poorer. You will understand the advantages available for business entrepreneurs compared to what consumers are entitled to and taxes they pay to support business entrepreneurs!

This is a simple system and requires time and patience. Once this part is done you are now ready to begin setting up your accounting books.

Country	1	2	3	4	5	6	7	8	9	10	11	12	1	2	3	4	5	6	7	8	9	10	11	12
Australia																								
Canada																								
Hongkong																								
India																								
China																								
Germany																								
Portugal																								
Taiwan																								
Egypt																								
Ireland																								
Japan																								
New Zealand																								
Pakistan																								
Singapore																								
Sweden																								
United Arab Emirates																								
United Kingdom																								
United States																								
Country Month	J	F	M	A	M	J	J	A	S	O	N	D	J	F	M	A	M	J	J	A	S	O	N	D

Chart of Various Fiscal Years

CHAPTER 7

Strategic Point No. 2

Planning

**"Reduce your plan to writing.
The moment you complete this, you will have definitely given concrete form to the intangible desire"**

-Napoleon Hill-

The planning process is more in-depth and can be looked at in different angles to what will be described here. However, use this as an outline to create a boundary so you can get started immediately.

By definition, ***planning is a vital aspect of any new, established or continual business development.*** Without planning you would not be able to connect your dots, place the puzzle together of your vision, and do your due diligence before committing to any venture.

Your time is the capital needed to invest in future success..........

Without your time to plan you can pretty much bank on the fact that you will not succeed.

You may be thinking *is there seriously a way to start a business and run a business and do it all on a shoestring budget?* I have to say, *'yes'*. It is so much easier than we have been led to believe. Many entrepreneurs believe that you need hundreds or even thousands of dollars to get a start in small business. The truth of the matter is that you need not much more than a good idea and lots of contacts and resources.

If you haven't yet decided what type of business you want to open, try looking around at what you have and what you know how to do..........

The most successful small businesses start with the owner's hobby and develop from there. Most people who enjoy sewing already own all the materials needed to start a small sewing business. Most people who enjoy programming computers already own the necessary equipment for this business. Take a look at what you already own and go from there.

Start with what you have.........

For example if you want to start a lawn care business, start with the lawn mower you already own. You can purchase a larger mower later, once you have started and have some cash flow. But for the time being, start with what you own.

Of course you can start some kinds of businesses with no capital. Service businesses tend to need a lot less capital than product businesses. Professional service businesses such as graphic arts, management consulting, engineering consulting, accounting and similar businesses don't need a lot of capital.

With no capital, you will not be able to open a physical storefront or an office outside of your home..........

Instead, you will need to use space already available to you in your own home. Some people are lucky enough to have an entire room available for their use in operating a small business. If you have space, put it to work, if not, create space.

Many businesses require no more than a desk and some storage space......

A small desk and a file cabinet can occupy a small section of any available room, a corner of the bedroom perhaps, or even the living room or dining room! It helps you to learn how to run a business creatively, turning you into a savvy entrepreneur.

Starting and running a small business is not just about working for yourself, it's also about having the necessary management skills, industry expertise, technical skills, finance and of course a long-term vision to grow and succeed.

Low budget advertising is the best source of marketing, it is free!

Word of mouth is usually cited as the best way to obtain new clients or customers. Ask every customer to refer you to at least one or two friends.

Joining local business groups is another great way to market your business.........

These groups provide plenty of networking opportunities and get the word out about your business.

Most importantly, mention your business at every opportunity - when chatting with friends, when meeting new people, when visiting family. Don't be shy! If possible, bring an example of your work with you everywhere you go. You never know when you will meet an interested potential customer! Get shirts made up with a business logo, be a walking advertisement for your business.

Capital – Do you need it?

If capital is needed, then my suggestions are below:

1. **Bootstrap**. Do it a little smaller. Use the money you make to fund a slightly larger part of the business and over time you can move into the original idea.

2. **Borrow** money from commercial sources (banks) or friends and family.

3. **Partner** with a company that would be providing one component of the business and start it as a joint venture. For example, if it's a web-based business, a web designer might partner with the person who has the knowledge about the subject of the website.

4. **Business Plan.** Whatever you do, going as far as you can alone, will determine how much of the business you will eventually own. A business plan and a prototype or mock up would be rock bottom minimum requirements.

5. **Use what money you do have wisely.** Before every purchase, ask yourself if the item you're about to purchase will really help you grow your business and if you can really afford it at this point. Don't be afraid to put off any purchases

until you've been able to consider it for a week or more.

There are lots more choices to consider, but the bottom line is that ideas are pretty much worthless without the ability to put them into operation. This means not only money, but the skills to implement the idea. If you have both 'idea' and 'skills' you should be able to create a good business plan and possibly drawings or a mock up for a product.

A real prototype might require more money than you might have. ***With good detailed drawings and a business plan, one might be able to find an investor or a partner.*** With just an idea, there isn't much hope in attracting an investor or a business partner, you need to take action and speed of Implementation is the key.

CHAPTER 8

Strategic Point No. 3

Objectives

"A set definite objective must be established if we are to accomplish anything in a big way"

-John McDonald-

The ***objective*** is to now obtain either a free download of accounting software from the Tax Office or a free 30-90 day trial version of MYOB or QuickBooks.

These sites can be very helpful especially if this is your first time registering and running a business:

www.dummies.com On this site you can download the book "Bookkeeping for Dummies", this will give you the understanding of Assets, Liabilities, Equity, Profit and Loss. Develop your intellect and gain understanding, because to end up managing your business you must understand the basics to making profit.

www.myob.com On this site you can down load MYOB Accounting Trial Version. The help menu is available to assist with setup, however, I personally find that www.dummies.com has the better book "MYOB for

Dummies", its explanations, are very simple and palatable.

www.quicken.com On this site you can download QuickBooks Trial Version and again go to www.dummies.com and download their book "QuickBooks for Dummies". This was the best investment I ever made!

Should you strike problems and still require someone to hold your hand through this process I would be inclined to go to www.youtube.com and in the search box place ***"MYOB Tutorials"*** or ***"QuickBooks Tutorials".*** These videos will definitely play an important role to cementing your understanding.

Now that you have your skeleton in place you need to start applying muscle around it to support the frame. These are called **activities** which we will go into at length in the next chapter. We all know that each part of the body has a function, so you must ensure each attribute of the body is finely tuned and correctly in place to move forward in the best possible way.

Five (5) Point Strategy to Establishing Your Footprint:

1. Look up your competitors (if any) in your local area, town or suburb you are living in on the presumption the area, or suburb has a mixed industry of commercial, industrial and residential

buildings. Send a fax or phone them enquiring of their fees for services.

2. Look up your local paper and see who if anyone is advertising a similar business to your idea.

3. Again enquire of what they offer for services.

4. Contact your local paper and let them know that you have started a new business and ask if they could run an editorial on you when they next have availability. Editorials are normally free, but can only be fit in, in order of enquiries and generally you find real estate agents normally get a piece of the pie first because of the financial investment they make in advertising. Never the less they will want to promote you because they will endeavour to gain your business in the long run.

5. By this stage your planning process should include tools, implements that are required for your business venture. These tools could be in the form of knowledge, experience, a lawnmower, different class of driving licences etc. This will automatically compliment your natural foundation, combined with your dream-seed which you are passionate about, and then your

tools will come in handy for performing the service.

Compile all the information you receive and work out a strategy to offer ***value*** for your service.

For Example:

If you are passionate about owning your own Cleaning Business, then consider promoting yourself using organic or natural products. Your highlight could be to promote the use of vinegar or natural citric acid from say oranges. For example eco-orange a product that combines technology and ecology providing solutions for all cleaning needs formulated with orange oils and enzymes containing only alkaline builders and biodegradable surfactants.

Next, extend your service contracts to not only domestic homes, but also commercial buildings, and perhaps target child care centres and banks.

With promoting domestic services such as lawn care, make sure to offer value by watering the plants and pruning lightly or taking away debris. *End each domestic service with a* ***"wow"*** *factor,* for example, placing a vase of fresh flowers before departure, if you are a Cleaning Business.

Now prepare a flyer using a word document, place your logo, contact details, business registration number and document your services. Print a large quantity and spend a few days exercising by doing letterbox drops. Otherwise you can pay a nominal fee and take the flyers to your local post office and they will place them in the P.O Boxes for you.

Next, I would take the flyer and pin it up on community boards around the suburb or local area. You will find that each area has neighbourhood community halls, notice boards and in shopping centres there is normally a notice board as well as clubs and places of gatherings etc...look for them and you will be surprised how many you find.

Lastly I would manually look up the local phone directory, not the directory for the state but for the local area which is usually printed for the particular districts, shires or counties. *Select the commercial businesses you would like to target for offering your services and fax through your flyer once a week for 3 months.*

To get through the door, offer a trial service free of charge or directly speak to the office manager.

Be confident and passionate when offering your services. Prospective clientele always pick up on the energy and drive you portray through your voice and body language.

Now that you have your foot in the door, remember in a local area, town or suburb it is always word of mouth that promotes your advertising not the flyers! If you were contracted to clean for a domestic home that has a young family, can you imagine how many other mothers would hear of your services while standing in the parking lot waiting to pick up their kids after school. The key ingredient *to keeping long term clients* and not just having today customers is to *show a heart of service*. I like to call it a servant-hood heart. You are in this business not only because it was your vision and dream-seed and passion, but because you sincerely have seen a lack of good quality valuable service whereby you have filled the void and become the solution to people's problems.

This is called enterprising!

Enterprise creates the solution. It is marked by an independent energetic spirit, imagination, initiative and boldness to undertake new projects, being very able, and ingenious in business dealings, and have a readiness to embark on bold new ventures. Is this you?

Once you take action, you can recreate another project and off you go again. Having multiple streams of income from different sources is the key to financial freedom and fulfilment. The biggest mistake a lot of entrepreneurs do is start a business and run it for more than 3 years without bringing the vision back to the table and streamlining the process by assessing it.

Re-visiting your services and competitors...

Adapting to surrounding changes such as growth of a suburb or industry, types of demographic shifting into and out of the area and most importantly economic growth and how it affects your clients' is vitally important if you want to stay ahead of the game.

You will not get caught out with the lack of work when financial crisis hits all around you because you have your dream-seeds positioned to adapt to change and are attentive to clients' needs because you have made it that their business is your business, their concerns are your concerns, and their needs are met with your solutions. You become a decision maker, a pillar of support, a platform for clients to depend on so they can be released to do what they are best at.

I applied the above methodology with my created bookkeeping business and reaped a large harvest within the first 12 months. Within 24 months I had employed three staff, and within 36 months I had five staff working for me. After running for three years it was time to shift gears because I was growing rapidly and my expenses were increasing, my demographic clients were changing because of the transient area I lived in and the needs were increasing for blue collar workers and less white collar workers.

My business was created by fax's being sent through to a select 32 businesses in the area and from there, word of mouth carried my business from strength to strength.

Apply diligence, focus, determination, loyalty and commitment to any person, be it a client or partner, and you will receive respect and favour in return.........

It is called the Law of Creation, or as some know it, the Law of Attraction. If you attract the right people you will be better for it. We are created to work together and help each other, promote one another and that is the Law of Creation. "What goes around comes around", you may have heard this phrase. You may have heard this biblical phrase, "what you sow you reap". We are in it for service to each other and gain from each other, and that's why networking with the right people allows you to cultivate your environment and establish your roots with credibility and honour.

If you think about the whole world and what services are required, it is a mammoth task to know exactly what is required, and when. It is definitely a service that is needed to help fellow mankind to achieve their personal dreams, so you and I, come to the rescue.

Summary Pointers – Time To Take Action....

1. **Know what you want to do –** stepping blindly into the business arena without a plan is suicide. Formulate your idea, research, look at statistics and know exactly where you want your business to go and what you want it to grow into.

2. **Be passionate** – if you don't LOVE what you are doing, everything (including family) will fall in a heap around you. Balancing your work life with your family is an amazing juggling act worthy of a medal! But if you are passionate about your work, you will be able to integrate it into your life more easily.

3. **Shamelessly self promote** – I harp on about this endlessly, but there it is, if you don't get out there and promote your business through every means possible, then you are doing yourself a disservice. Promote through passive marketing (flyers on noticeboards), networking (with networks and at events) and to the media. Start off locally and then spread your wings nationally and internationally. Please note: make your story sound newsworthy and not like an advertisement, or you will be sent advertising rates and that is definitely NOT what you want. You want free publicity.

4. **Get yourself a Mentor** – someone who can cheer you on when things are going great and hold your *hand when the going gets tough. I can't stress enough how important it is to have someone in your life who has been there and done that who can help you in your business journey.*

   Just having a person you admire and respect to run things by and talk to is worth its weight in gold. Now what you need to do is get out there, work hard and believe in yourself. Passionate people can achieve amazing things in the business world, make your mark and set your blueprint!

CHAPTER 9

Strategic Point No. 4

Activities

**"Plan your progress carefully,
hour-by-hour,
day-by-day,
month-by-month.
Organised activity and maintained enthusiasm are the well springs of your power"**

-Paul J Meyer-

1. Meet and Greet Clients, don't rent an office! Work from home, or better yet work from the best free office with locations everywhere? Gloria Jean's, Starbucks, or any CBD (central business district) Cafes. If you need to meet with a client and are worried about seeming small not having a professional office, don't be. Just meet them at a restaurant for a lunch meeting. This is what people with the nicest offices do anyway.

2. Don't hire any employees! Do it all yourself until you have some dollars coming in the door.

Legal Stuff and Registrations

3. If you need a lawyer, get a free lawyer and legal advice from the mentors at www.caxton.org.au or www.score.org. You can also do a Google search for free legal advice in your country and generally you will find that these organisations are government funded through grants.

4. Initial accounting consultations are generally free. Accounting firms want to secure you as a client for years to come, especially if they see the passion and potential, they will be willing to give free advice before incorporating your enterprise.

5. A Proprietary Limited Company (P/L) or Liability Limited Company (LLC) is probably the best business structure, but do not worry about incorporating a company yet, run a sole trading proprietorship, you can always incorporate later.

6. Learn how to do your own Financial Statements by using Excel, MYOB or QuickBooks. If you download the free version of MYOB, in the reporting section you can print a template for your Profit and Loss (PnL), Balance Sheet and export it to Excel. Now you have an accounting based spreadsheet regardless if your free trial has ended or not.

7. Download Youtube video Tutorials if you get stuck with an accounting program.

Make a website for your business

8. Register a domain www.domain.com , www.godaddy.com, www.register.com make sure to pick a domain name with one keyword in it. To clarify, a **keyword phrase** is generally two or more words that are used by advertisers in search engine optimization (SEO), or by visitors who are using search engines in a desire to find information based on that particular phrase. For example, an advertiser that sells blue carrot shoes might use "blue carrot shoes" as a keyword phrase to draw more visitors interested in the topic, which would then match the keyword phrase with websites like that of the advertiser that mention the same keyword phrase. Assuming it is not a very competitive keyword you will rank on the first page of Google within a month or two for that keyword – which means "customers".

9. Test out your ideas by writing to a blog, you'll get feedback on what people like and don't like.

10. Get a free business website at www.wordpress.com or www.tumbler.com or www.weebly.com or www.wix.com or www.knowem.com . It won't be your own domain it will be something like 'yourbiz.wordpress.com' once your domain is registered add this as a custom domain to your Word Press or whichever site you choose to register with.

11. Get a professional website design for free with Word Press theme www.wpthemeland.com, you can install with a few clicks, no programming knowledge is needed.

Get a Logo

12. Don't hire a fancy graphic designer. At least not yet, use www.logoyes.com to create your own logo or if you want to spend $5.00 to have your logo created for you, then go to www.fiverr.com

Accepting Payments - Credit Cards

13. Don't bother with a full merchant account to start off with. They are complicated, come with monthly fees, and require programming expertise. Instead, you may try a simpler and much cheaper solution such as www.checkout.google.com or www.paypal.com .

14. For a more professional look and a complete shopping cart, for only $5.00 per month, use www.e-junkie.com

15. If you have lots of physical products for sale, you may want to try a Yahoo Store such as www.smallbusinessyahoo.com/ecommerce

Starting a service business where you train, consult, coach, teach, etc.

16. Create several pages on your Word Press site www.wordpress.com one for your experience, testimonials, rates, availability, etc.

Creating Information Products

17. You could use a free e-book template from www.ezebooktemplates.com, www.ebooktemplatesource.com, www.ebookhelper.com.

18. For print books, self-publish it at www.lulu.com and use print on demand. They don't print a single book until someone buys it which means you have zero upfront cost for inventory!

19. Use a $20 webcam or digital camera to create educational video products.

20. Use **Camtasia** for PC or iShowU for Mac to record your screen and make great videos or record Power Points and do the voiceover to make great educational products or even better use **ScreenToaster** which is a free online screen recorder.

It is free screen recorder *software* used to record your screen. It is a free web based screen recorder, so you do not need to download or install anything!

Screen Toaster can be used to record screen casts, tutorials, etc. You can also embed the videos on blogs and websites or email it to a friend.

21. Use a Mac to edit your videos - iMovie is free and you can even produce DVD's.

Before investing in a retail location...

22. Go to your local markets, local fair or festival and rent a booth to see if anyone buys your product. Talk to potential customers and get feedback.

23. Try selling it on eBay.

Always be learning about business

24. Go to a www.meetup.com, groups in your city related to business/entrepreneurship. Contact the Chamber of Commerce in your area, Small Business Association, which provides free and low-cost advice on every aspect of your business, including the licenses you may need to operate, the tax and insurance considerations.

25. Read all the best business books by getting them from the library.

26. Get three of the top ten books on building wealth for free in PDF, just Google it and download.

27. Make friends with other entrepreneurs and share material.

28. Install the www.stumbleupon.com toolbar and choose business/entrepreneurship as one of your interests to find all the best videos and talks out there, this is literally like going to a free business school, you get to see all the best speakers and thinkers of our time, and those of the past.

Marketing - FREE Website Traffic and getting your first customer

29. Get 250 full-colour business cards from www.vistaprint.com/free-businesscards.aspx for free to hand out to people you meet.

30. Post videos on You Tube with links to your website.

31. Post the same video to all video sharing sites, Google Video, Yahoo Video, MySpace, Revver, etc at once with www.tubemogul.com this is some of the best free marketing you can do!

32. Generate leads by offering an incentive on your website for people to give you their contact info. Examples of some incentives that work well are *Top 10 reports like the top 10 myths about…the top 10 thing you should know before…, videos, audio interviews, one page cheat sheets, free e-Books.*

33. Learn how to use Google Ad words www.adwords.google.com, spend $10 and see if it brings in at least $10 if so keep going!

34. Get links to your site by using Directory Submitter www.freewebsubmission.com to obtain hundreds of smaller links from directories for free.

35. Google *"on page SEO"* and do some basic simple 10 steps. A keyword analysis is an early, critical step in search engine optimization (SEO.) It's the difference between guessing what your prospects are searching for and knowing what they are searching for.

How to do some basic SEO? Or how do you find out what people are searching for?

36. The first step is to generate/brainstorm a list of key phrases. I often recommend approaching the brainstorming session with five perspectives in mind, including,

- products and services
- prospects, problems or pain points
- actual or perceived benefits
- features
- competition

37. Research what keywords will bring you the most traffic and are least competitive. Keyword Discovery www.keyworddiscovery.com, and Wordtracker www.freekeywords.wordtracker.com, teach you to target your audience with the right keywords.

38. Get more incoming links to your site by creating a Squidoo page www.squidoo.com these rank very highly in the search engines.

39. Send an email to everyone in your email program's contact list with a short friendly note letting them know you are starting a business and ask if they could forward it to just one or two people who might be interested. Offer something free for the first 10 people. This has an exponential effect because it not only reaches who you know, but everyone who knows who you know.

Lastly to conclude this Activities Chapter, put yourself on Facebook, LinkedIn, and Twitter, if you haven't already. Those are all free avenues for finding customers.

CHAPTER 10

Strategic Point No. 5

Tasks

"The secret of getting ahead is getting started. The secret of getting started is breaking your overwhelming tasks into small manageable tasks, and then starting on the first one"

-Mark Twain-

Go through a simple exercise of putting a few things on paper for your own good. Describe your business in one sentence, preferably eighteen (18) words or less.

Tasks:

1. *Who will buy your products or service?*
2. *How much money do you absolutely need to get started?*
3. *How much can you realistically charge for your product or service?*
4. *What will it cost you to deliver that product or service?*
5. *In the worst-case scenario, how much can you make?*

Don't assume the best-case scenario because more often than not, you won't meet those projections. A baker may dream of selling 100 cakes a week, but is five more realistic to start? A dog walker might assume he can handle 10 customers a week, but is two more realistic to start?

Know the competition:

Don't worry about reinventing the wheel. This is all about rinsing and repeating and again repeating and rinsing! Chances are you are going to provide a service or product that already exists. That's OK. There are multiple banks, coffee shops, clothing stores and restaurants on every street. There are thousands of doctors and dentists in every major city.

It's wise to know your competition, but don't be intimidated, especially if you offer a quality product or service, and an extra ***"wow"*** service!

Create marketing materials. You need a marketing plan to target the right people about your business. Because you aren't going to run expensive newspaper ads or commercials, think free and inexpensive.

Website, when you're looking to buy something from a haircut to a custom cake you likely will hit the

Internet. So even if you're not selling online, every business should have a Website.

Google's Ad Words program is an affordable and measurable way to attract visitors to your Web site. Sign up for free and set a budget for how much you want to spend to appear in search results when Google users look for content related to yours.

Network, this is a must! Relation Capital is a vital aspect and role, and creates cash flow which is the blood line to any enterprise.

For printing your business cards and flyers try www.vistaprint.com, www.clickbusinesscards.com or www.gotprint.com for the look of high-quality printing at affordable prices.

Phone system, assign and designate your mobile phone as your direct contact.

Use free social and business networks. Facebook, LinkedIn, MySpace and others are valuable tools for spreading the word about your business.

Establish mutually beneficial partnerships. For example, if you are an animal lover, and have an enterprise in the industry, then partner with the most popular pet store in the area to host in-store events every Saturday where owners could bring their animals for on-the-spot mini massages. It is good for the store because it brings new and existing customers into the shop, and it's good for attracting brand awareness and customers alike for this new pet massage business.

By the same token a cake baker might offer to do fundraisers for a school. They could talk to wedding vendors about offering affordable alternatives to new brides. They can visit local coffee shops with samples of the baked goods to persuade them to carry the varieties.

Generating free media coverage by using www.helpareporter.com, enables anyone to sign up for a free e-mail alert, delivered three times daily, listing the immediate needs of writers and producers from major TV and print outlets to blogs and books. By registering for the daily emails, you can respond to queries from journalists that relate to your business and your expertise without hiring a publicist to do the work for you.

Find Free Resources!

Find free helping hands. When you have little to no money to start, you have to be resourceful to get as much as you can for free. In addition to begging family and friends, contact colleges in your area to post internship opportunities for students who would welcome a compelling role in assisting with your start-up.

Tap into free expert resources. We mentioned this earlier in the previous chapter, contact the Chamber of Commerce in your area, Small Business Association which provides free and low-cost advice on every aspect of your business, including the licenses you may need to operate and the tax and insurance considerations.

Expand your knowledge globally and learn from other countries of how they market themselves, aim to establish an eminence with your enterprise. I am a proud Australian, however I love to glean from other nations because they have been established far longer than our 200 years of existence. Check-out these sites which provide expert information. Start Up Nation www.startupnation.com, Small business Television www.itsyourbiz.com, and Collective-E www.collective-e.com

Finally, just do it! If you can't get out there and sell your product or service, you won't have a business. It doesn't matter how fabulous your offer, your expertise or your website is, if nobody will pay you for it. Get your ducks in a row and then get in front of your target audience. Nobody will have the same passion and enthusiasm as you. Your passion is priceless!

Partnerships, *Do's* and *Don'ts*

Whether you are starting a business or running an existing business, you don't need to get money from investors to make it a success..........

You can find potential partners everywhere. They're online and they're down the street. The same person who would laugh you out of their office if you asked them for a $2,500 investment may gladly trade $2,500 of their services to be part of a promising new venture. Why? Like you, most people are looking for an opportunity to get ahead without risking too much. If someone can invest a little of their time with the hopes of making a huge return, they may jump at the chance. Plus, it's much less painful than trying to get money from Uncle Harry!

The solution is to get the business off the ground, through partners or suppliers who are willing to trust and invest in your idea before the cash comes in. Here are some tips on how to tap into your network, use the most powerful capital of all, ***relationships.***

1. Money is not the only form of capital.....

Many entrepreneurs have started their business by forming alliances and partnerships with people who specialize in the resource that they need.

Think about it this way. You have an area of expertise, for example baking amazing cookies. You have a wonderful recipe that you know could topple Mrs. Fields' or Betty Crocker Cookie Empire. This is a resource, another resource is time, and you have plenty of hours to devote to your business.

There are other people who may have money, but would rather not get into the nitty gritty of starting and running a bakery. So don't say *"you don't have anything."* You do! You're not going around asking for freebies or help. You're looking for an exchange of capital, a chance to share in your business idea and your time, in exchange for money to expand it.

2. Look for people who need what you have.....

Don't go to a friend and say, *"Hey, can I borrow money for a business?"* Instead you can say, *"I have a business idea, and it could potentially earn* 'xxxx'*a month, far more than what you would earn by putting money in a bank."* Or, *"You've been talking about quitting your job, but worrying about a regular source of income. What if you invest in my business? I'll build it while you work, and it may one day reach a point when you can quit your job and still have a good source of income."*

3. Trade resources.....

Let's say you need a website, but can't afford a programmer. Why not approach a website team and offer something in exchange? For example, if you're good at marketing, you can design high-quality brochures for their own sales efforts. Or you can offer space on the website where they can put their ads, *"this website was designed by..."*

The most effective trade, however, is when you partner with someone based on a business' future success. *"Help me build this business and make it grow, and you'll earn far more in the long run."*

4. Build the idea.....

You are securing resources on the basis of trust, and the only way to earn trust is to have a solid business idea. Work out the business plan and all the details, logistics, market, competition, etc. You could run informal conversations regarding demographics, economic impacts and ideas with friends, business associates, relatives, neighbours asking their opinion so you can fine tune the proposal and tell your investors, *"People said they would pay xx for this kind of product."*

5. Prepare a compelling presentation....

Invest your time in creating a powerful presentation. Make a mock-up of the product in its packaging. Think out and write a script that is brief, factual, and presents your idea in the best possible light and end the presentation with a concrete offer. Don't just say, ***"I hope you invest."*** This is too abstract and people will easily forget or waffle about. Give figures or specific ways of involvement: ***"If you come in as a full***

partner, you will get..." or ***"If you provide this type of service, you will get..."***

Having concrete partnership packages also protects you, because the business document helps you manage the other person's level of involvement in your business.

One Last Word....

This book presents invaluable information for people seeking to make a difference through financial objectives to create wealth. These objectives then become a personal vision, a dream-seed. To activate this vision requires a set goal and plan that includes implementation of specific business strategies. These strategies require processes and tools amenable to periodic reassessments that will no doubt, adequately accommodate market fluctuations to ensure business sustainability.

I am often asked the question," What is success?". Most definitions include references to achieving goals and acquiring wealth, prestige, favor and power. Successful people enjoy the good life by being financially and emotionally secure, being surrounded by admirers, and enjoying the fruits of their labours.

Successful people are leaders, opinion makers, and trendsetters. Their example is emulated and their accomplishments are noticed. They know who they are and where they are going, and they stride confidently to meet their goals.

So I challenge you today to step out, step up, and see your dreams turn into reality. Together we can make a difference in our world.

> ***"Goals are means to an end, not the ultimate purpose of our lives, they are simply a tool to concentrate our focus and move us in a direction. The only reason we really pursue goals is to cause ourselves to expand and grow"***
>
> **Anthony Robbins**

EXAMPLES of Starting Up Your Own Business

Web Hosting: This is indeed one of the easiest businesses to start right now. With little or no capital, you can pick up a reseller plan from a reliable web hosting provider from within your location. Visit, **Start a Profitable Web Hosting Company** for details, there are many sites offering this service, Google it and choose what is right for you.

Web designer: This is one niche where there is high demand right now. You only need to have the basic skills and should be able to work with PHP and MySQL. You will also be able to get many clients if you can design custom Word Press themes. The starting point is for you to create a blog for yourself to show what you can do. You may also need to join forums where you can easily market your skills to others.

Consultancy: Helping other people run their business may seem daunting at first, but many budding entrepreneurs have the skills and experience to become first class consultants. I'm not an electrical engineer, but I have to assume you can start your own business as an electrical engineer for hire, as a consultant, without needing much more than your expertise and credentials. Will your business require equipment such as a computer? Will you need a marketing budget? You might, but then again you might be able to start your consulting business simply by calling a few contacts and getting hired.

Clothes shop: With such a wide range of clothes shops out there, you have several options when trying to tap into this huge market.

Outside catering: Whether it is catering for a major sporting event or a low-key wedding, the need for food and drink at gatherings does not go out of fashion. Find out how to set up your own catering company.

Gift shop: Boosted by the tourist trade, gift shops can be a very popular business to own. Why not get wrapped up in the idea and start up your own? Remember Valentine, Easter, Mothers Day, Fathers Day, Christmas is around the corner. You may be able to make some money...

Driving school: Whether it took you two attempts or 20 to pass your driving test, you wouldn't have got there without a driving instructor. If you can put up with the exams and novice drivers, this line of work can be rewarding.

Photography business: When your school photo was being taken, you probably gave little thought to the fact that the photographer would soon be off to another job, maybe a wedding, to make ends meet. If you have a passion for photography, get a clear picture of what is involved in setting up your own enterprise.

Day nursery: With both parents increasingly keen to return to work after having children, day nurseries are also vital to many families who can't afford to give up a regular income to stay at home. You really need to network and let people know that you are available for this. You are definitely going to make some money from this if you manage it well.

Restaurant: Whether you are celebrating a special occasion or just don't fancy cooking, eating out is big business with a huge variety of restaurants. This is one business you should consider starting if you have the required capital.

Bookkeeping: Get registered with the relevant government bodies or associations, and promote yourself by attaching a covering letter and your Resume', either faxing it or emailing the details to small business enterprises such as service or trade industries, consultancies or franchises. Follow up with a phone call.

Lawn mowing: Do you have a lawnmower? Do you love gardening? Do you take pride in a manicured lawn? Do you have a car? Do you have a box trailer? Do you have all the necessary tools for gardening? Then what are you waiting for?

Driving License: Have you ever thought of running a private taxi-limo service? Get a license to drive a taxi. Start this process at the Department of Motor Vehicles. To drive a taxi, a particular license is required. The name of this license varies from state to state. Find out if your town regulates taxis. Determine who licenses the taxi companies and off you go!

Mat Cleaning Business: Have you ever wondered who cleans the mats that you walk on when you enter a shop? Or, the runners in the shopping centre and the plastic rubber mats that scrape the gravel and mud off your shoes before you enter a restaurant or place of worship? To promote longevity for these client investments, the mats need to be maintained by washing them weekly by transporting them to a commercial Laundromat. You can offer the service of pick up and drop off, charging per item dictated by size. You can even go to the extent of using a pressure cleaner to clean the mats and you can dry them in the sun. This is a niche service if worked right.

Teach: What qualifications do you have? Are you an Engineer, a Music Teacher, a Mechanic, a Botanist, a Doctor, a Beauty Technician? Whatever your trade or skill is, offer your services to your local community and offer to be a mobile service.

Leather lounge Solutions: this is an enterprise of demand. We all want a leather lounge but hate cleaning them because they never come up looking right. Get the experts in who spend lots of time polishing your furniture to make it look immaculate, conditions and adds longevity.

ABOUT THE AUTHOR

Business Enterprise Coach,
Speaker, Mentor & Author

Grace Evans has led an extraordinary life. At a very young age she created, wrote, directed and performed in a play which incorporated 100 actors at a National Theatre in the Capital City of Khartoum, Sudan. In addition, having no prior experience, Grace raised the capital to fund this venture. The success of this first enterprise made a profit of 500%! This became her seminal moment as it proved to her that dreams are the inspiration which transform a vision into reality and can have a tangible reward.

This experience gave Grace a special insight, and at the age of 19 she was running a small business adding 200% to its bottom line in the first month. Her ability to recognize which areas of a business to concentrate on and what strategies to employ to ensure minimum effort for maximum gain led her into bigger and better things. Grace continued to build her skill sets, knowledge and mastery of leadership by joining Dun & Bradstreet, beginning her ascent in the corporate world.

With the ability to create multiple enterprises, Grace has established a number of businesses in the fields of:

Finance, Business Consulting and Training, Trades Industry, Shipwrights, Professional Consultancies, Real Estate, Offshore Investments and South Pacific Ventures.

Grace has a unique ability to seek out and capitalize on emerging trends in niche markets, helping many clients to do the same.

As an Inspirational speaker Grace combines her driving passion and commitment to help up and coming entrepreneurs, allowing them to achieve their desires and fulfil their God given destiny. Grace trains, equips, mentors and coaches those who are willing to step out and step up to transform their visions, ideas, dreams and desires into realities!

Grace Evans is truly a gift to those who seek to find direction, transform their thinking and master their destiny! If you have the Passion! Grace will provide the Direction!

www.youdontneedcapital.com

Made in the USA
Monee, IL
04 November 2026

67375832R00059